La Girona

Loch Tay

The Lusitania

The Vasa

Antikythera

The Mary Rose

Yassi Ada

Cape Gelidonya

Apollonia

The Nuestra Senora de la Concepcion

Madrague de Giens

The Geldermalsen

The Batavia

THE SEARCH FOR
SUNKEN TREASURE

Nicola Barber and Anita Ganeri

Macdonald Young Books

T R E A S U R E   H U N T E R S

First published in Great Britain in 1997 by Macdonald Young Books
an imprint of Wayland Publishers Limited

© Macdonald Young Books 1997

Macdonald Young Books
61 Western Road
Hove
East Sussex
BN3 1JD

Find Macdonald on the internet at http://www.wayland.co.uk

Concept Designer: Jane Hannath
Designer and Typesetter: Kudos
Illustrator: Mike White
Map Illustrator: Bruce Hogarth, David Lewis Agency
Map Calligraphy: Oriol Bath, David Lewis Agency
Commissioning Editor: Fiona Courtenay-Thompson
Project Editor: Caroline Arthur
Assistant Editor: Lisa Edwards
Series Editor: Nicola Barber

Photograph Acknowledgements: AKG photo p.37(ct); Ancient Art and Architecture
p.11(br); Bridgeman p.11(ct), 25(tr); C.M.Dixon p.14(bl)(tr), 15(c); Christie's p.22
(bl)(br), 23(bl); Fortean p.41(br); Hulton Getty p.25(bl); Mary Evans p.8(cl)(tr),
43(tc)(c); Mary Rose Trust p.29(br), 30(cl); Photri p.36(bl); Planet Earth p.12(tr),
20(bl)(br), 21(bl)(cr)(br), 26(cb), 39(tl); Rex Features p.38(cb); Scottish Trust for
Underwater Archaeology p.17(bl)(cr); South American Pictures p.34(bl); Topham
p.30(bl), 31(tr)(cb), 33(tr), 36(cb), 41(tr); Ulster Museum p.33(br); Wayland p.29(tl).

Picture Researcher: Shelley Noronha

Printed in Hong Kong by Wing King Tong

A CIP catalogue record for this book
is available from the British Library

ISBN: 0 7500 2245 0
*Image for the artwork on p.16 supplied by the
Scottish Trust for Underwater Archaeology*

CONTENTS

INTRODUCTION

When you think of sunken treasure, you probably conjure up a picture of a shipwreck lying on the sea bed, with its cargo of gold and silver scattered around it. This is what a few treasure hunters have been lucky enough to discover. But shipwrecks are not the only 'treasures' that lie under the waves. Less glamorous underwater finds can be just as exciting and revealing.

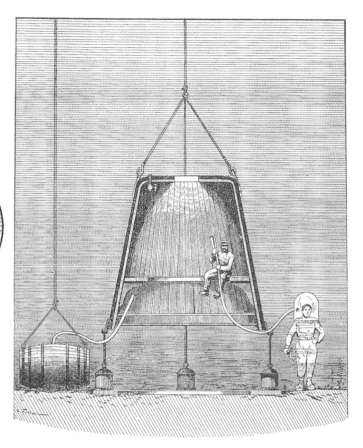

Edmund Halley's diving bell. Fresh air was lowered down to the sea bed in barrels. The air was fed by tube into the bell, and then through another tube to the diver. The diver wore a head covering called a 'cap of maintenance'.

According to legend, Alexander the Great was lowered into the Bosphorus Sea in one of the first diving bells.

GOING UNDER WATER

For centuries, divers have braved the sea to look for beautiful corals, sponges or pearls. In about 450 BC, the Greek historian Herodotus described how two divers swam down to recover treasure from a warship that had sunk in the Mediterranean Sea. In the seventeenth century AD, Spanish settlers in the Caribbean sent local divers down to their wrecked ship (see page 20). Of course, these divers could stay under water only as long as they could hold their breath – the record was five minutes!

Divers needed to be able to spend more time under the water, so inventors started to experiment with diving bells containing air. In 1717, the British astronomer Edmund Halley made a diving bell with leather tubes to supply air to the diver. Then, in the 1830s, the first diving suits were developed. These were heavy rubber suits with large copper helmets. The suits and helmets were not completely watertight, but the air pressure inside the helmet kept the water below chin level. These suits allowed divers to go deeper and to dive for longer, but they also made life more dangerous.

The bends

As divers go deeper and deeper below the surface, the weight of water pressing down onto them increases. This extra pressure produces bubbles of gas in their blood. If a diver then comes back to the surface of the water very rapidly, these bubbles of gas block the nerve endings causing swellings, terrible pain and even death. This is called 'the bends' or 'diver's disease'. The only remedy is for the diver to go back to the increased pressure, for example, a special room with high air pressure, and to come back to normal pressure very slowly, so that the blood can re-absorb the gas bubbles.

Before anything was known about 'the bends', many divers died. In 1878, the disease was explained, and charts began to be made showing how long divers could safely stay below the surface.

The invention of scuba diving equipment in the 1940s revolutionized underwater archaeology.

LAKE NEMI

One of the earliest attempts at underwater archaeology was made in Italy during the 1440s. A collector of Greek and Italian art, Cardinal Colonna, heard about two ancient Roman ships which were said to lie at the bottom of a lake near Rome. Swimmers who were sent down to find the ships reported that they were indeed there, 18 metres below the surface. But it was 500 years before anyone was able to salvage them. In 1932, the lake was drained to expose the two ships, and they were finally brought onto dry land – only to be burnt to cinders when German troops invaded in 1944!

Scuba

The big breakthrough in diving technology was made in the 1940s by the underwater explorer Jacques Yves Cousteau. He developed 'scuba' (self-contained underwater breathing apparatus). The diver does not need to wear a suit, but carries cylinders of compressed air which are strapped to the back. Tubes run from these cylinders to the mouth, and valves control the air pressure.

Interest in underwater archaeology has increased as new ways of excavating, filming, taking photographs, surveying and recovering objects from under the water have been developed. Treasure hunters and archaeologists have explored countless shipwrecks, as well as the remains of drowned villages, harbours and towns. This book tells the stories of just a few of these explorations around the world.

ANCIENT WRECKS

The position of the wrecks described in this chapter

One evening in October 1900, a group of Greek fishermen were sailing home after a hard day's work diving for sponges. Suddenly, they were caught in bad weather. The captain, Dimitrios Kondos, decided to take shelter near the small island of Antikythera. When the storm had died down, Captain Kondos sent a diver to search for sponges. The man put on his heavy metal helmet and rubber suit, then went down to the sea bed. But after only a few minutes he resurfaced, seeming very excited. As soon as he could speak, he babbled a confused story about horses, men and naked women he had seen on the sea floor!

A SPONGE DIVER'S DISCOVERY

Captain Kondos could make little sense of what the frightened diver was saying, so he decided to go and look for himself. He put on his diving suit and swam down 55 metres to the sea bed. When he returned to the boat, he was clutching a bronze arm. The horses and people at the bottom of the sea were statues: the diver had discovered an ancient wreck.

After making a careful note of the position of the wreck, Captain Kondos and his crew returned home. They tried to keep their discovery a secret, but the story soon leaked out. By law, Captain Kondos had to tell the Greek government about his find, so when he realized that the news was spreading like wildfire he contacted the Greek minister of culture.

Captain Kondos' diver found ancient bronze and stone statues on the sea bed.

Giant statues

The sponge divers went back to Antikythera in November. This time they had a naval ship with hoisting equipment to help them lift the statues off the sea bed. One of the first objects to break the surface of the sea was a bronze head, now known as the 'philosopher's head'. This was followed by the bronze arm of a boxer, a bronze sword, two stone statues and many fragments of statues and pieces of pottery. But the most sensational of all the finds was a complete bronze statue of a youth. Archaeologists were amazed at what a good condition this was in, considering it was over 5,000 years old and had lain at the bottom of the sea for more than 2,000 years!

Salvaging the statues was very hard work for the divers. Their suits were heavy and awkward, and each diver could do only two or three five-minute dives in a day. To make matters worse, several statues seemed to be lying beneath some huge pieces of stone. These stones would have to be moved if the statues were to be salvaged. The divers passed thick cables around each stone, and one by one the ship towed them to deeper water and dropped them there. Suddenly, the archaeologist on board the naval ship had a terrible thought. What if these 'stones' were not stones at all, but huge statues? The next stone was hauled to the surface, and sure enough it was a gigantic statue of Hercules, dressed in a lion skin and carrying a club. The other 'stones', now well out of reach in deep water, were probably huge statues too.

The 'philosopher's head' was one of the first objects brought to the surface from the Antikythera wreck. The head is made from bronze and dates from the third century BC.

A wonderful treasure trove

By the end of 1901, the divers had discovered a huge amount of treasure. The finds included statues, wine jars (called amphoras), pottery plates, glass vessels, roof tiles and a gold brooch decorated with pearls. All these finds were taken to the National Museum in Athens, where they were examined by experts. Some wooden planks from the ship's side were also recovered from the sea bed.

At that time, both the archaeologists and the divers viewed the wrecked ship simply as a wonderful treasure trove. The archaeologists were not interested in studying the remains on the sea bed, or in talking to the divers about what they saw there. As far as they were concerned, the divers' job was to bring the treasures to the surface. Certainly, none of the archaeologists involved in the Antikythera excavation could dive themselves. They seemed to be there mainly to make sure that the precious artefacts were not stolen.

THE ANTIKYTHERA 'COMPUTER'

One of the most exciting finds from the Antikythera wreck was almost ignored altogether. Nearly a year after the dive had finished, one of the archaeologists noticed a lump of corroded bronze among the finds. The lump looked as though it might be a clock or some kind of instrument for navigation. Finally, in 1971, when scientists were able to X-ray it, they found out that it was a device used to calculate the positions of the sun, moon and stars. This amazing 'computer' was made in about 87 BC.

11

Underwater Archaeology

Until the 1950s, all underwater exploration was done by divers, with archaeologists supervising from ships on the surface. But then an American diver, Peter Throckmorton, decided to follow up a lifelong interest in archaeology, and an American archaeologist, George Bass, decided to learn to dive. Bass had some exciting new ideas about underwater archaeology. He believed that an archaeologist should be in charge of all parts of the excavation, and that it should be carried out as carefully and thoroughly as an excavation on land.

The two men met up in 1960 to excavate a shipwreck site off Cape Gelidonya in southern Turkey. Their aim was to teach people who had experience on archaeological digs to dive, rather than trying to teach divers to excavate the site. George Bass explained to the team how he wanted to carry out the excavation. First, they would make an accurate plan of the shipwreck as it lay on the sea bed, carefully noting and labelling all the objects. Only then could the divers begin to bring artefacts to the surface. From all the evidence – drawings and photographs of objects on the sea bed, and the objects themselves – it was possible to piece together the story of the ship and the people on board. This was the beginning of modern underwater archaeology.

The story of the Gelidonya ship

In about 1200 BC, a merchant ship from Phoenicia was sailing westwards towards the Aegean Sea. Its last port of call had been Cyprus. Here, the crew had loaded on board a cargo of scrap metal – copper, bronze, tin and lead. As the ship rounded Cape Gelidonya, it hit some underwater rocks and sank in about 27 metres of water.

The Phoenicians lived along the coast of present-day Lebanon. They were good sailors, who travelled the length of the Mediterranean. They exported cedar wood cut from the forested mountain slopes near their cities, exotic oils and purple-dyed cloth. The Phoenicians set up trading posts and colonies

This diver is bringing an amphora (jar) to the surface. It is partly covered with marine growths.

along the coast of North Africa, in Sicily and Sardinia, and at Gadir (Cadiz) in the south of Spain.

Wrecks at Yassi Ada

In 1961, George Bass went on to excavate another wreck, this time off Yassi Ada, a small island south-west of Turkey. In fact, there were several wrecks at this site, but Bass decided to concentrate on 'wreck number three', which lay about 37 metres below the surface. The excavation itself lasted four years. But it took fifteen years for the archaeologists to study the maps, photographs and drawings of the site, and all the finds!

Many of the objects that the divers found on the Yassi Ada wreck were shapeless lumps. Each lump was carefully labelled and its position was noted. When the lumps were brought to the surface, they were found to be more interesting than they looked. If iron objects are left for a long time in the waters of the Mediterranean, they quickly become covered in growths (tiny marine plants and animals). Over the centuries, these growths become thicker and thicker, while the iron inside rusts away, leaving a hollow

Divers used lifting balloons to retrieve objects from the Yassi Ada ship.

COUSTEAU AND GRAND CONGLOUE

In 1952, a team of divers led by the Frenchman Jacques Cousteau worked on a wreck found at Grand Congloué near Marseille, in France. This was the first time a pump was used to remove sand and mud from a wreck. Cousteau also designed and built a platform from which the divers could work in any weather. Cousteau and his divers recovered vast amounts of material, but they were not trained to make sense of what they saw on the sea bed. Nor were the finds labelled or recorded. It was only many years later that archaeologists sorted out the evidence and realized that there were in fact two wrecks at Grand Congloué, and that the second had sunk up to 100 years after the first.

space. When Bass and his team cut the lumps in two and filled the spaces with rubber, they ended up with perfect models of the original iron objects. They found the ship's carpenter's tools – an axe, a hammer, chisels, knives, nails and tacks – as well as the nails and bolts that were used to hold the ship's hull together.

From clues on the sea bed, another archaeologist put together a picture of how the ship would have looked. It was a Byzantine merchant ship, and it sank in around AD 626. It was about 21 metres long and 5 metres wide. We even know the name of the ship's captain, from inscriptions on objects found on the ship: Georgios Presbyteros Naukleros, 'George the Elder, senior sea captain'.

The inscription 'Georgios Presbyteros Naukleros' was found on a steelyard on board the Yassi Ada ship. A steelyard was a kind of balance, used to weigh objects.

ANCIENT PACKAGING

The wreck discovered by George Bass at Yassi Ada contained over 900 amphoras. The other wrecks nearby were also excavated, and they too had cargoes of amphoras. What were these jars used for?

In ancient times, the amphora was simply a kind of packaging. Just as today we use glass or plastic containers to protect and transport food, so people around the Mediterranean used amphoras as containers for products such as wine, olive oil, fish and a kind of fish paste called *garum*. Amphoras were made from rough clay, and the insides were rubbed with oil or rosin to make them waterproof.

This mosaic from Ostia in Italy shows an amphora being unloaded from a larger sea-going ship (right) to a smaller ship. The smaller ship will take the cargo of amphoras up the River Tiber to Rome.

They often had pointed bottoms and handles on either side, although the design depended on where and when the amphoras were made.

Some amphoras have the name of the amphora-maker scratched into the clay. Others were stamped with the name of the wine-maker whose wine was being transported. All these clues have helped archaeologists to build up a picture of the busy trade in wine and other goods around the Mediterranean.

Madrague de Giens

One of the biggest ancient wrecks ever excavated was at Madrague de Giens, near Toulon in southern France. This wreck turned out to be a Roman wine ship dating from 70–50 BC, which could have carried between 6,000 and 7,000 amphoras. Divers found hundreds of amphoras still neatly stacked in the cargo hold; traces of rushes and heather showed that they were once cushioned against the movement of the sea by layers of packing.

Some of the amphoras were marked with the name of the maker, P. VEVEIUS PAPUS. Archaeologists know that his workshop was south of Rome, in the region called Latium. Some of the wine came from this area, too, from the famous vineyards in Caecubum. We know this because the clay seals in the tops of many of the amphoras have the vineyard-owners' stamps on them.

Amphoras from an Ancient Roman wreck. They have pointed bottoms to make them easier to stack into the hull of a ship.

MARBLE CARGOES

Rome was famous throughout the ancient world for its grand buildings. The first emperor of the Roman Empire, Augustus, boasted that when he came to power Rome was a brick-built city, but that he left it covered in marble. Marble was highly prized by the Romans, but where did it come from, and how did it get to Rome?

The answer is that marble came from all over the vast Roman Empire, and that it was brought to Rome by sea. Some of the blocks of marble transported from far-off lands to Rome were so huge that special ships had to be built to carry them. Needless to say, quite a few of these 'marble ships' ended up under the waves, their cargoes scattered across the sea bed.

Excavation of these shipwrecks has helped historians to piece together quite a good picture of how the Roman marble trade worked. For example, one wreck of a Roman ship from the third century AD contained marble blocks from quarries in central Asia Minor (present-day Turkey), which had been ordered for a building or monument in Rome. Some of these blocks were rough and uncut, others were carved and almost finished. There was an altar, some basins and even a sculpture. Obviously, there were craftspeople working at the quarry, who were sent instructions from far-away Rome. It's possible that the craftspeople even travelled to Rome to complete the carving and polishing there.

The marble head of a horse, brought up from the sea bed near Greece.

FLESH-EATING STONE

Wealthy Romans liked to be buried in stone coffins, known as sarcophagi. The word 'sarcophagus' comes from the kind of stone often used for these coffins. This stone was quarried in Asia Minor, and the Romans believed it consumed the flesh from the dead person's bones. Its name, Lapis Sarcophagus, means 'flesh-eating stone'!

A sarcophagus was a stone coffin with a lid. These coffins were often highly carved and decorated.

HOUSES OVER THE WATER

One of the most exciting things about underwater excavations is that objects which do not survive on land, because they are exposed to the air, are often amazingly well preserved in water. On these pages, we travel to the cold, dark, peaty waters of a Scottish lake, or loch, to look at the story of some unusual houses, called crannogs.

THE CRANNOGS OF SCOTLAND AND IRELAND

'Crannog' is a Gaelic word used by the people of Scotland and Ireland to describe houses built on artificial islands surrounded by water. The remains of crannogs have been found in lochs, in marshes, and in shallow bays and estuaries. Crannogs have a very long history. People probably started living in them as early as 5,000 years ago, and crannogs were still being built in the seventeenth century AD. Since crannogs were usually made from wood, they have decayed over time, and none has survived intact. We know about them today because archaeologists have gone underwater to study crannog remains around Scotland and Ireland.

What did a crannog look like?

One of the first people to become interested in crannogs in Scotland was a doctor called Robert Munro. He heard about the exciting finds in Switzerland (see box), and spent two years travelling around Scotland, noting down what he found at crannog sites. In 1882, he published a book called *Ancient Scottish Lake Dwellings or Crannogs*. For years, this was almost the only information about crannogs. People assumed that there were only a few of them in Scotland, and that they were mainly in the south-west, where Dr Munro lived and did many of his excavations.

A reconstruction of the crannog at Oakbank, Loch Tay, Scotland

In 1953, a crannog was excavated in Milton Loch. From the evidence that was discovered, the archaeologists made drawings of this crannog. These show a round hut with a thatched roof and wickerwork sides, built on a wooden platform which is supported by thick tree trunks driven into the soft mud of the loch bottom. Many people still think of this as a typical crannog.

More recently, archaeologists have found out that there are many more crannog sites in Scotland than they once thought – probably over 1,000. And the round, thatched hut was not the only type of crannog. Some crannogs were rectangular, some were joined to the shore by causeways, and others had small docks for boats instead.

Why build over water?

Why did people go to the trouble of building houses in the middle of the water? The likely answer is that it was usually for safety. Some crannogs were built as far out towards the middle of a loch as possible, well away from any danger. Others were nearer the shore, close to good farming land. Some crannogs were built to keep animals out of harm's way; others were places for hunters to spend the night. Crannogs also seem to have been good hideaways: after the unsuccesful uprising against the English in 1745, some of the Scottish rebels took refuge in crannogs.

A butter dish found at Oakbank in Loch Tay. The red numbers show where the remains of 2,500-year-old butter were found sticking to the dish!

Underwater finds

The cold, peaty waters of Scottish lochs preserve many fragile objects that would not survive in the open air. Archaeologists have found wooden cups and spoons, combs and pins made from bone, and even tiny pieces of cloth, buried in layers of mud. At Oakbank crannog in Loch Tay, archaeologists found the bracken and ferns spread on a house floor by Bronze Age people, as well as pottery with burnt food sticking to it and a butter dish with butter in it. At another crannog site, in Loch Bharabhat, on the Hebridean island of Lewis, archaeologists found a wooden carving of the head of an animal. None of these objects would have survived in such good condition in the air.

An archaeologist excavates a wooden bowl from beneath the waters of Loch Tay. The bowl was found underneath a timber post on the bed of the loch.

ALPINE 'STILT VILLAGES'

In the 1850s, a schoolteacher made an exciting find on the shores of Lake Zurich in Switzerland. The level of the water in the lake had dropped, and part of the lake bed along the shoreline had dried out. Some wooden posts were sticking out of the mud, and nearby there were many old artefacts. At the time, archaeologists said that these were the remains of a prehistoric stilt village, built over the water on wooden platforms. However, research this century has shown that the village was in fact built beside the lake, not over it. The level of water in the lake has risen over time and covered the village.

SALVAGING TREASURE

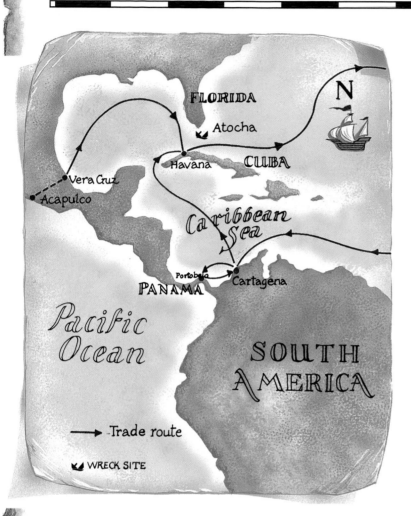

The routes of the Spanish treasure fleets and the position of the *Atocha* wreck

'**At seven in the morning he saw ...**
Nuestra Señora de Atocha ...
dismasted except for the mizzen mast. While he watched, she went down and ... nothing could be seen of the ship.' This is how one eye-witness reported the last few minutes of the Spanish treasure galleon, the *Atocha*, before it disappeared under the waves off the Florida coast in September 1622. On board the *Atocha* when it sank were 260 crew and passengers, and vast amounts of gold and silver treasure.

HIDDEN DANGERS

For centuries, ships were the safest and fastest method of transporting valuable goods around the world. But, as the story of the *Atocha* shows, sea travel could be risky. This Spanish galleon was only one of thousands of ships that went to the sea bed taking their precious cargoes and unfortunate crews with them. Surprisingly, most shipwrecks happened not in the open sea, but near the coast, where sand banks, rocks and reefs lurked unseen beneath the waves. As we shall see, some routes were particularly dangerous.

The treasure fleets

The *Atocha* was one of a fleet of twenty-eight ships, the great 'treasure fleet' which sailed between Spain and the Caribbean every year. On the outward journey from Spain, the ships of the treasure fleet carried tools, weapons, cooking equipment, clothes, wine and food – everything that the settlers in the Spanish colonies in Central and South America might need. On the return journey, the ships' holds contained vast riches. When the Spaniards had invaded Central and South America in the 1530s, they had found a seemingly endless supply of gold and silver. The job of the treasure fleet was to transport this wealth back across the Atlantic Ocean to Europe. The ships also carried emeralds and other gemstones, pearls and exotic products such as tobacco.

None of the sailors on the treasure fleet ships would have looked forward to the journey home from the Caribbean. The route was terribly dangerous. Late summer was the hurricane season, when violent storms could strike at any time. There were deadly underwater reefs along many shorelines, particularly off the Florida coast. Pirates lay in wait to attack the fleet. Even worse, the ships were often old and unseaworthy, and the crews were sometimes inexperienced. It is not surprising that about fifteen per cent of all the treasure loaded onto the Spanish ships ended up on the sea bed.

Nuestra Señora de Atocha

At Portobelo and Cartagena, the *Atocha* was loaded with ingots (bars) of gold and silver. The official register shows that the cargo included 161 gold ingots and 901 of silver, thousands of silver coins and large numbers of uncut emeralds. On board the *Atocha* were several wealthy Spanish officials and merchants, returning home with valuable jewellery and other gold and silver artefacts. The ship also carried supplies of tobacco, rosewood, a blue dye called indigo and ingots of copper from Cuba.

The fleet set sail from Havana, in Cuba, on 4 September 1622, but within two days a violent hurricane scattered the ships. The *Atocha* and its sister ship the *Santa Margarita* were both wrecked on the reefs off the Florida Keys. Only five people were rescued from the *Atocha*. Seven of the twenty-eight ships in the fleet were wrecked. The rest managed to sail back to Havana for repairs, and to report the dreadful loss of life – and of the treasure.

The *Atocha* and the *Santa Margarita* disappear beneath the waves.

19

The salvage operation

The Spanish officials in Havana were horrified at the loss. They made a plan to salvage as much treasure as possible from the ship. The *Atocha* had gone straight to the ocean floor without breaking up, and one of its masts was sticking out above the water, so there was no difficulty in finding the wreck. A boat was sent to the area, with a team of divers on board.

These divers were local people, who usually made a living finding pearls in the waters around the Caribbean islands. They could swim down to depths of 30 metres, clutching large rocks to help them sink quickly to the sea bed. Often, they stayed under water for up to five minutes before coming up for air! But when the divers swam down to the *Atocha*, they discovered that the portholes and hatches into the cargo hold were firmly locked, so they could not reach the gold and silver ingots. They managed to rescue only two bronze cannons before another storm hit the area and the salvage boat was forced back to harbour.

When the divers returned to try again, the mast had gone, and so had the buoys left to mark the position of the wreck. The waves had broken up the ship, scattering the treasure across the sea bed. The Spanish salvage team never managed to find the *Atocha,* and in time the ship and its fabulous treasure were forgotten . . .

Local divers tried to reach the *Atocha*'s precious cargo, but the portholes and hatches were firmly locked.

Many priceless treasures were lost with the *Atocha*, including a pearl-studded cross and chains (above), and a solid gold cup and plate (right and far right).

Diving for treasure

. . . Until the 1960s, that is, when a treasure hunter, Mel Fisher, began to look for the *Atocha* and its sister ship, the *Santa Margarita*. At first, he did not make much progress, but then he teamed up with a historian, Eugene Lyon, who was very good at making sense of historical documents. In an old Spanish document, Lyon found a description of the place where the *Atocha* sank. After sixteen years of searching, Mel Fisher and his team finally made a breakthrough on 20 July 1985, when they found a stack of silver ingots on the sea bed. The wreckage was scattered across the ocean floor about 11 kilometres from where the ship had first sunk.

An archaeologist worked with Fisher's team, recording the position of the remains of the *Atocha*'s hull and of its scattered cargo. When the treasures were eventually brought to to the surface, everyone knew that the sixteen years' hard work had all been worth it. The finds included gold chains, a jewel-encrusted belt, an emerald-and-gold cross and ring, and many other priceless objects.

THE CONCEPCION

Another trade route that was often used by Spanish galleons ran across the Pacific Ocean, from Manila in the Philippines to Acapulco on the west coast of Mexico in Central America. The goods were then taken overland from Acapulco to Veracruz, on the east coast, where they were loaded onto the treasure fleets to be transported to Europe. What cargo did these Pacific galleons carry? At the wreck site of the Nuestra Señora de la Concepción, *which sank off the Mariana Islands in 1638, divers found spices such as cinnamon, pepper and cloves, thousands of pieces of broken porcelain, and jewellery set with precious stones. The ship probably also carried cotton cloth from India and Chinese silks.*

More treasures from the *Atocha*: the jewel-encrusted belt (above) and gold ingots and chains (below)

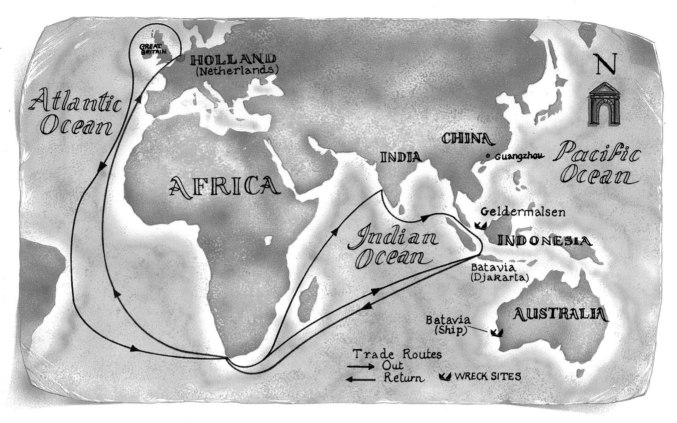

The routes taken by the ships of the East India Companies and the wreck sites

THE EAST INDIA COMPANIES

While Spanish galleons sailed across the Atlantic and Pacific oceans, explorers from other European countries were investigating different sea routes to the riches of the East. Both the Dutch and the English set up East India Companies in the early 1600s. The aim of these companies was to develop trade with India and the 'Spice Islands' (in present-day Indonesia). On the outward journey, the ships of the East India Companies carried gold and silver to trade for goods, as well as supplies for the companies' trading posts. On the way back, their holds were stuffed with spices of all kinds, silks and perfumes, carpets, gemstones, tea and porcelain. We know from written records that many East India ships were wrecked in storms, or ran aground on reefs, but only a few wreck sites have been found. One of these wrecks is famous for its amazing cargo.

22

The Nanking cargo

The Nanking cargo is a collection of about 160,000 porcelain objects. The collection is made up of cups, saucers, plates, bowls, beer mugs, soup dishes, butter dishes and vomit pots. The cargo was discovered in 1985 by a team led by the diver Mike Hatcher. It was eventually sold by the auctioneers Christies, fetching over ten million pounds.

Surprisingly, the Nanking porcelain was not the most important part of the cargo carried by the Dutch ship *Geldermalsen*. When the ship left the port of Guangzhou, China, in December 1751, it was carrying a valuable cargo of tea. This would have been worth more than ten times as much as the porcelain if any of it had ever reached Europe. The tea was packed in tin-lined wooden boxes at the top of the ship's hold, with the porcelain in crates underneath. The porcelain was not of particularly good quality, either. It was mass-produced in potteries in China, and was intended for sale in Holland, where tea-drinking had become a fashionable craze.

THE BATAVIA

Like the Geldermalsen, *the* Batavia *was a ship belonging to the Dutch East India Company. It was wrecked off the western coast of Australia in June 1629. When divers excavated the wreck site in the 1960s, they came across some building blocks made from sandstone. These blocks seemed to be shaped and carved. Once they were on dry land, archaeologists pieced them together – rather like a giant jigsaw puzzle! They formed an impressive doorway, probably intended for the East India Company's headquarters in Batavia, Indonesia.*

The end of the Geldermalsen

The *Geldermalsen* came to grief on a reef in the South China Sea in 1752. Apart from the tea, there was another precious cargo on board – gold bars. One of the few sailors who survived the shipwreck told the following story. As waves began to lap over the deck, the captain ordered him to carry a heavy chest up from below. Just as he was about to swing the chest out onto one of the lifeboats, the *Geldermalsen* finally sank. The sailor was saved, but the chest disappeared beneath the waves. Over 200 years later, it was found by Mike Hatcher's divers, lying a small distance from the wreck itself. It seems that the sailor's tale was true.

Part of the Nanking cargo: a dish (far left) and tureen (left), and part of a 316-piece dinner set (above)

TREASURE HUNTERS AND ARCHAEOLOGISTS

Some people criticized the way that Mike Hatcher salvaged the cargo from the wreck of the Geldermalsen. *Professional treasure hunters need to work quickly when they find wrecks, and there is not much time for careful archaeological work. But without the efforts of treasure hunters such as Mel Fisher and Mike Hatcher, many wrecks would simply never be found. Archaeologists have only recently realized how important underwater finds can be. Water preserves wood, leather and even food, so a shipwreck is like a time capsule, where everything remains exactly as it was at the moment when the ship went to the bottom of the sea. The best way to explore shipwrecks is probably for professional treasure hunters and archaeologists to work together, as they did on the* Atocha *excavation.*

DROWNED SETTLEMENTS

Throughout history, there have been many tales of whole cities, ports and harbours which have sunk beneath the waves. What were these settlements like? When did they fall into the sea, and why? What can they tell us about life in the past? This is the story of one of the most famous sunken cities of them all, the notorious pirate harbour of Port Royal, Jamaica, which, on 7 June 1692, dramatically slumped into the sea.

The pirate city of Port Royal, on Jamaica's south coast

THE PORT ROYAL DISASTER

It was just before noon, and the city of Port Royal, on the south coast of Jamaica, lay basking in the midday heat. In the harbour, cargo was being unloaded from a ship. Elsewhere, a group of sailors ambled down Thames Street, on their way to the cookhouse for lunch. Then, all of a sudden, the ground began to shudder. From the mountains behind the town came a hollow, rumbling noise, like thunder. A violent tremor shook the ground, then another and another. It was a massive and disastrous earthquake.

Before the eyes of the city's terrified inhabitants, the whole of the waterfront, including Thames Street, slid into the sea. Houses and shops crumbled and disappeared into the gigantic, yawning cracks that tore open the ground. The people tried to run away, but it was too late. According to one eye-witness, 'the earth heaved and swelled like the rolling billows'. A huge tidal wave swept in from the sea, drowning the parts of the city that were still left standing. Within the space of two short minutes, the sea had swallowed two thirds of the city, and 2,000 people were dead. The city never recovered. It was 'shaken and shattered to pieces, sunk and covered by the sea'.

THE PIRATE CITY

In the seventeenth century, Port Royal lived up to its description as 'the world's wickedest city'. Because it stood at one of the busiest points on the trade routes between Europe and the Americas, it made an ideal headquarters for pirates. From this port, with its fine harbour and well-fortified shores, the pirates made attacks on the Spanish galleons carrying gold and silver from the Caribbean to Europe. The city grew rich on their plunder, and its people spent much of their time gambling and drinking rum in the dozens of taverns which lined the streets.

Most of the pirates' ill-gotten gains were sold off to the city's merchants. Their warehouses overflowed with gold and silver, fabulous jewels, silks and rich brocades, all waiting to be shipped to Europe in exchange for money and other goods.

Port Royal reached the height of its fame under the notorious Sir Henry Morgan, one of the fiercest pirates of all, whose reputation for murder and robbery was second to none. By the time of the disaster, Morgan had been dead for four years. Although he was buried in the cemetery on the waterfront at Port Royal, this was not his final resting place. When the ground heaved and the sea rolled in, the cemetery vanished beneath the waves, taking Henry Morgan with it.

A pamphlet describing the terrible events of 7 June 1692

Ripe for plunder

The city's merchants were horrified at the loss of their precious belongings. Almost immediately after the earthquake, they hired divers to search the drowned city. Large quantities of goods and riches were recovered using grappling hooks, nets and poles – the only salvage tools there were at the time – but much more was out of reach. For hundreds of years, this vast treasure trove lay under the water, just waiting to be found. With its hundreds of houses, shops, taverns and warehouses, and the ships which sank in the harbour, Port Royal was surely one of the richest archaeological sites in the world.

Sir Henry Morgan, one of the most feared pirates of all, was buried in the cemetery at Port Royal.

Modern treasure hunters

In 1959, *Sea Diver*, an American ship built especially for underwater exploration and equipped with radar and echo sounders, sailed to the site of Port Royal. Although most of the site was less than 18 metres beneath the surface, the water was so clouded with silt and sand that the divers could barely see. It was difficult work, and there was also the danger of the rubble caving in on them. Despite this, in two months of diving, the members of the expedition found hundreds of objects. On the sea bed were the remains of brick walls, which the divers uncovered using water jets and an airlift (a huge tube which works like a giant vacuum cleaner to suck up finds or debris and carry them to the surface). Buried under the silt, they found not only the remains of houses, but also thousands of wine bottles, clay pipes, candlesticks, guns, and pewter cups, plates and spoons. There was even a copper cooking pot containing beef and turtle bones, the ghostly remains of someone's final meal, abandoned when the earthquake struck.

TELLING THE TIME

One of the most fascinating artefacts found among the sunken ruins of Port Royal was a gleaming brass pocket watch, made in Holland in about 1686. The glass was missing and the watch face was covered in a thick, black crust, but the insides were as good as new. When an X-ray was taken of the face, the archaeologists were even more excited. For the X-ray showed traces of the watch's lost hands, which had stopped at 11.43 am, precisely the time of the earthquake!

The amazing brass pocket watch found at the site

A vast selection of pewter jugs, plates, bowls and spoons was found under the sea.

More excavations

The next big excavation of Port Royal took place from 1965 to 1968, and was led by the archaeologist Robert Marx. He had to work as quickly as possible, because there was a plan to build a new deep-water port on the site. (This would have destroyed over half of the sunken city, but the plan was later cancelled.) To start with, progress was slow in the cloudy water. The divers had to spend many hours removing tonnes of modern rubbish and debris from the sea bed. Beneath this there were layers of silt, mud and coral. Gradually, a large area was cleared and mapped, and thousands of finds, large and small, were airlifted to the surface. These came from a group of about thirty or forty buildings under the water.

By checking the owners' initials stamped on silver and pewter objects against the written records, Marx was able to identify these buildings. Most were private houses, but several were taverns. There was also a carpenter's shop, a cobbler's shop, a pewter-smith's shop and the city's fish and meat markets. The divers recovered over 100,000 artefacts, including pipes and bottles, huge quantities of pewterware, cannons and ship's fittings. Most exciting of all was a wooden chest, which crumbled as soon as they touched it, leaving only a brass lock and key and its contents – hundreds of freshly minted silver coins.

And yet the project covered only five per cent of the whole sunken city. Who knows how many more thousands of objects lie buried beneath the waves?

Finding a wooden chest full of silver coins was the most thrilling moment of Robert Marx's excavations.

SUNKEN HARBOUR

Earthquakes, tidal waves and a rising sea level brought doom to many ancient harbours along the Mediterranean coast. The Greek port of Apollonia in Libya was built in about 631 BC. Today, its ruined remains lie several metres under water. Archaeologists have worked out that the harbour was surrounded by islands connected by massive stone breakwaters. At one end, divers found a large fish tank, with dividing walls and sluices to control the water flow. They also discovered the ruins of buildings which once stood on land, such as grain stores, warehouses, taverns and rest houses for the sailors. But nobody really knows why Apollonia slid into the sea. Did an earthquake cause the harbour to tilt? Or was the sea level lower when the harbour was built?

Sunken Warships

The *Mary Rose* sank off Portsmouth on 19 July 1545.

The sea is dangerous at the best of times, but for warships the risks are even greater. Over the centuries, battles and storms have destroyed hundreds of warships, some of whose wrecks have been found off coasts around the world. Many more remain undisturbed and undiscovered. Who knows what fabulous treasures they contain? These are the stories of some of the most famous shipwrecked warships of the past – King Henry VIII's favourite ship, the *Mary Rose*, and the doomed galleons of the Spanish Armada.

The crowd in the harbour watched in horror as the ship went down. Many had friends and relations on board.

Going to War

It was 19 July 1545. England and France were at war, and an invasion fleet of 200 French ships waited, ready for battle, off the Isle of Wight. At nearby Portsmouth, King Henry VIII watched as the wind changed and the English navy was at last able to sail along the coast and out to meet the French. His mighty flagship, the *Great Harry*, led the charge, closely followed by his favourite warship, the *Mary Rose*.

From the battlements of Southsea Castle, the king and his courtiers had a clear view of the action. Below them were thousands of soldiers, ready to fight any invaders who managed to make it to the shore. The *Mary Rose* fired one broadside at the enemy ships, then turned sharply so that the guns on its other side could fire. Its lower gun ports, just above the water, were open and ready for action. Then came disaster! Before the horrified eyes of the crowd, the ship dipped sharply, and water rushed into the open gun ports. In an instant, the *Mary Rose* rolled over and started to sink. The cries of the drowning crew carried across the water. One of the onlookers, Lady Carew, fainted into a courtier's arms – her husband was on board. Of the 700 soldiers and sailors on the *Mary Rose* that day, fewer than forty men survived.

A painting of the *Mary Rose* as it may have looked on the day it sank. This picture was part of the Anthony Roll, a list of all Henry VIII's warships, drawn up in 1546. Recent excavations have shown that the actual ship looked rather different to this picture.

Royal favourite

Henry VIII began to strengthen the English navy soon after he came to the throne in 1509. He wanted it to be the most powerful in Europe, with the largest warships ever built. These would have more cannons and be better equipped for fighting. The 700-tonne *Mary Rose* was built in Portsmouth in 1509–10, and it was made entirely of oak. It was named after Henry's sister, Mary Tudor, and his family emblem, the rose. For thirty-five years, it was the pride of the fleet, a very successful warship. On that fateful day in 1545, it was carrying thirty-nine heavy bronze and iron cannons, together with thirty lighter cannons.

Nobody knows the exact cause of the disaster. Perhaps some of the cannons came loose and rolled around, making the ship more unstable as it turned. But witnesses told another story. No one seemed to be in overall charge of the ship, they said. Each of the sailors thought he knew best.

Almost immediately, Henry gave orders for the ship to be rescued. The navy, helped by a team of Italian divers, tried to raise the ship by the masts. But it was much too heavy for their salvage equipment, and they gave up. For more than 400 years, the *Mary Rose* lay on its side 14 metres down on the sea bed, almost totally forgotten.

LIFE ON BOARD

Thousands of military objects and personal belongings were found among the wreckage of the Mary Rose. *These included over sixty items used by the ship's surgeon, a skilled doctor, who was always busy preventing the spread of disease among the crew and tending battle wounds. In a large wooden chest in his cabin, divers found wooden pots containing ointments and peppercorns (for treating fevers), two metal syringes, razors and the handles of several surgical instruments. His cabin was near to the main gun deck, so that he was always close by when the ship went into battle.*

The surgeon's chest from the *Mary Rose*

Rediscovering the Mary Rose

In 1965, Alexander McKee, a naval historian and amateur diver, set out to find the wreck of the *Mary Rose*. He thought it was possible that the ship's hull, which had been buried in mud for 400 years, might not have rotted away. The search did not start well. But then McKee came across a chart, drawn in 1841 by earlier explorers, which marked the spot where the *Mary Rose* lay. Using sonar equipment, he and his team of divers explored the area shown on the map. Before very long, they found a wreck. But was this the *Mary Rose*? In 1970, divers dug an iron gun out of the mud. Sure enough, it came from King Henry VIII's favourite ship. The puzzle was solved.

Raising the Mary Rose

Shortly after the wreck was discovered, divers, archaeologists and scientists decided to work together to explore and survey the site. More than 10,000 objects were brought up from the sea bed, including the bones of about 100 sailors, guns, longbows and arrows, leather shoes, musical instruments, the ship's bell, pewter cups and plates, dice and dominoes. Many of these artefacts had been perfectly preserved by the mud and silt where they were buried.

In 1979, the Mary Rose Trust was formed to excavate the ship and its contents properly. Hundreds of volunteers took part. Between 1979 and 1982, every detail was recorded. Decks and cabins were brought ashore timber by timber, in preparation for the most exciting moment of all. On 11 October 1982, the wreck of the *Mary Rose* was finally raised from the sea bed.

Navigational instruments found on the *Mary Rose*. From left to right: a protractor, steering compasses and dividers. These were used to plot the ship's course on a chart.

CONSERVING A WRECK

Once an ancient wooden wreck, such as the Mary Rose, *is removed from the sea, scientists have to work quickly to protect its waterlogged timbers which will decay very rapidly in the air. Some wrecks are sprayed with a special chemical wax, called polyethylene glycol (PEG). This has to be done every day for at least ten years. The PEG replaces the water in the wood, so that when the timbers are eventually left to dry out they do not warp and shrink.*

The ship is now housed in a 'dry dock', on public view.

LOOKING FOR CLUES

Another great royal warship, the Vasa, *sank only hours after it was first launched, in August 1628. The ship was caught in a squall while still in Stockholm harbour. It turned out to be very unstable, and within minutes it capsized and sank. There were few survivors. Many of the ship's sixty-four guns were salvaged soon afterwards, but for over 300 years the* Vasa *itself lay stuck in the sea-bed mud. Then, in 1956, Anders Franzen, an amateur marine archaeologist, rediscovered it. A small but vital clue led him to the wreck. While he was collecting objects from the harbour floor one day, he found a piece of ancient, black oak. The* Vasa *lay about 35 metres down, almost perfectly preserved. It was raised in 1961, and is now in a specially built museum in Stockholm, looking much as it did on that fateful day in 1628.*

The reconstructed *Vasa*, on view in Stockholm, Sweden

This was not at all easy. The timbers that made up the ship's hull were very fragile and could not take any strain. So a steel frame was placed around the hull to give it support. Then the hull and frame were lifted into a steel cradle, which was the same shape as the hull and lined with airbags. The whole thing was then raised from the sea bed and towed into Portsmouth Harbour. Since then, the Mary Rose Trust has spent years restoring and conserving the ship. You can now see the *Mary Rose* for yourself and enjoy a fascinating glimpse of life on board a Tudor warship 450 years ago.

Lifting the hull of the *Mary Rose* inside a specially built steel cradle

Skirmishes and storms

The Armada came within sight of the south coast of England on 30 July. After several small battles with the English navy, it sailed to Calais, in northern France, to pick up more troops. While the Spanish were still at anchor, the English sent burning fireships in amongst them. At this, the Spanish fleet scattered in a panic, and the English attacked them fiercely, doing serious damage. To make matters worse, the Spanish troops at Calais were not yet ready, so invading England was impossible.

By now, fierce gales were blowing from the west, which meant the Armada could not return quickly to Spain along the English Channel. Instead, the ships had to go the long way round, sailing north around Scotland and Ireland. Here they were buffeted by terrible Atlantic storms, which blew them onto the rocky coast. Forty ships were wrecked, and another thirty were lost at sea. Only sixty limped home to Spain.

Driven off course by gale-force winds, half the ships in the Armada never made it home to Spain. They were blown onto the rocks and wrecked.

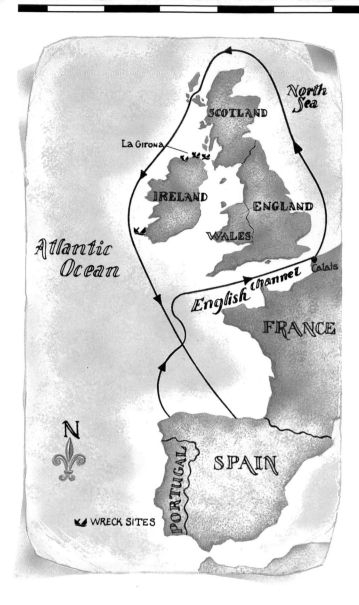

The route taken by the Armada ships and the sites of some of the most important wrecks

SAILING TO DEFEAT

In May 1588, King Philip II of Spain sent an enormous fleet to attack England, which was ruled by Queen Elizabeth I. The Spanish Armada consisted of 130 ships, including twenty-two huge galleons; on board were 2,431 guns, 8,000 sailors and 20,000 soldiers. The plan was to destroy the English navy, which had only about 100 ships, and to invade southern England. The Armada was the biggest fleet that had ever gone to war. But by the time it returned to Spain two thirds of the men were dead and over half of the ships had sunk.

La Girona

One of the wrecked ships was a galleass (a ship with both oars and sails) called *La Girona*. When his own ship and another one were wrecked, Don Alonso de Leiva, second-in-command of the whole Armada, transferred the survivors and a fortune in gold and silver onto *La Girona*. But, off the wild north coast of Ireland, *La Girona* also sank without trace. There were only five survivors out of over 1,000 people on board.

For almost 400 years, the wreck of *La Girona* lay undisturbed. But where was it? There was no record of the exact spot. Then, in 1967, a Belgian diver, Robert Stenuit, made an amazing discovery. He had spent many hours studying charts of *La Girona*'s last voyage and reading stories told by the ship's survivors. According to these, the ship had gone down in a small bay in County Antrim, which even today is called Port na Spaniagh (the Spanish Port). Stenuit was sure that this was the place, and he was right! On his very first dive, Stenuit found two bronze cannons and a copper coin. But more was to come. Washed into an underwater cave at the foot of the nearby cliffs, he found a treasure trove of gold and silver coins, golden chains and silver cutlery.

Divers raising a bronze cannon from the wreck of *La Girona*

GOLDEN TREASURES

It is said that the ships of the Armada fleet were carrying enough gold to pay all the soldiers and sailors and to cover the cost of the invasion. None of it ever returned to Spain. On its final voyage, La Girona *held the wealth of not just one Spanish galleon, but three. Divers have salvaged more than 12,000 artefacts from the wreck, including hundreds of gold coins, gold rings and chains, and other fabulous jewels. Among them were a beautiful golden cross, which belonged to Don Alonso de Leiva himself, and a wonderful golden salamander pendant, studded with rubies. There were also many ghostly reminders of everyday life, such as the leather soles of shoes and even plum stones.*

Many exquisite gold treasures were found in the wreck of *La Girona*.

33

THE SACRED WELL

According to the sixteenth-century Spanish writer Diego de Landa, in the city of Chichén Itzá, the capital of the Maya people of Central America, there was a large well. At times of drought or plague, the people of the city walked in procession to the well and threw in both rich treasures and human sacrifices. These offerings were made to please the rain god, Chac, who, they believed, was one of the gods living inside the well.

Chichén Itzá lies in the Yucatán region of Mexico.

THE SEARCH FOR THE WELL

About 300 years later, De Landa's words were read with excitement by a young American diplomat called Edward Herbert Thompson. Thompson later described his reaction to De Landa's story in his book *People of the Serpent*: 'From the moment I read the musty old volume, the thought of that grim old water pit and the wonderful objects that lay concealed within its depths became an obsession with me.'

When he was only twenty-five, Edward Thompson went to an area of Mexico known as the Yucatán, to work for the American consul. He was fascinated by the archaeology of the region, and after a few years he managed to buy the abandoned plantation where the ruins of the ancient city of Chichén Itzá stood. There he found the well, a huge oval shape 60 metres across. As he gazed down at the murky water about 20 metres below, Thompson was certain that De Landa's description of the ceremony at the well was true, even though most historians did not believe it. He thought up a daring plan to try to prove he was right.

Thompson took diving lessons, bought underwater equipment and arranged for a dredger and lifting gear to be set up next to the well. By throwing wooden logs that were about the same size and weight as a human being into the well, Thompson worked out roughly where the sacrificial victims might have landed in the water. This is where he began dredging.

The mysterious and murky waters of the sacred well at Chichén Itzá

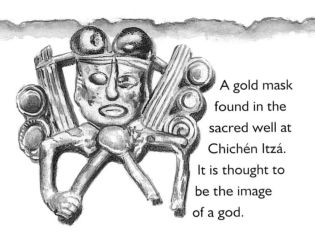

A gold mask found in the sacred well at Chichén Itzá. It is thought to be the image of a god.

IN UTTER DARKNESS

This is how Thompson described his first dive into the well, in his book People of the Serpent: *'During the first ten feet of descent, the light rays changed from yellow to green and then to a purplish black. After that I was in utter darkness. Sharp pains shot through my ears, because of the increasing air pressure . . . I felt a strange thrill when I realized that I was the only living being who had ever reached this place alive and expected to leave it again still living . . .'*

Right or wrong?

For days, the dredger brought up nothing but slimy mud, dead leaves and broken branches. Thompson began to give up hope. What if he was wrong, after all? Then, one morning, two dark objects lay amongst all the debris. At first, Thompson could not work out what they were. Then he broke one open, and a rich smell wafted out. They were balls of incense, which must have been thrown into the well during some kind of ceremony.

From then onwards, the dredger brought up all kinds of fascinating objects: pottery vessels, incense burners, pieces of jade, artefacts made from copper and gold, beads, and axes and hammers made from flint. Thompson had been right to believe De Landa's story.

Into the well

Eventually, the dredger stopped bringing up anything but a few sticks and leaves. Now it was time for Thompson to try out his new diving skills. He had managed to find two Greek sponge divers (see page 10) to help him with his task. As the three men climbed down the long ladder towards the thick green water below, the local workers solemnly said goodbye. They were sure that the three divers had made the gods of the well angry, and that they were on their way to a watery grave. But the explorers survived that first dive and many others over the next few weeks.

Deep in the well, the water was so dark and muddy that even the strongest flashlight was useless. The divers worked by feel, groping along the floor for crevices and cracks in the rock. They put anything interesting into a pouch and took it to the surface. The finds included more incense, jade, bronze and golden ornaments, and also three ceremonial knives. These had been used to cut out the hearts of the sacrifices thrown into the well. Thompson also found human remains: twenty-one skeletons of children, and twenty-one adult men and women.

The end of the story?

This was not the end of the story of the well. In the 1960s, archaeologists uncovered many more objects, including some sandals made from gold. Who knows what the sacred well may still have hidden in its murky depths?

Thompson oversees the dredging operation at the sacred well.

THE UNSINKABLE SHIP

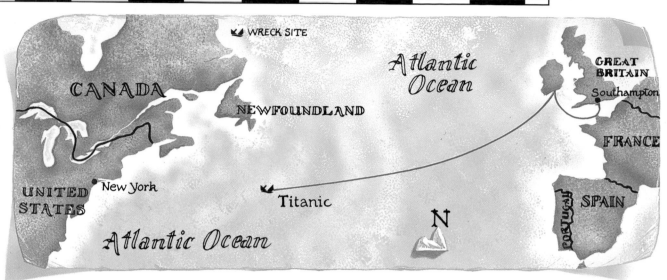

The route of the *Titanic*'s fateful maiden voyage

On the evening of Sunday, 14 April 1912, everything was quiet aboard RMS *Titanic*. The luxury liner, the greatest ship of its time, was on the fourth day of its maiden voyage, from Southampton, England, to New York, USA, with 2,201 people on board. The ship was built of the finest steel; its owners boasted that it was 'practically unsinkable'. It was commanded by Captain Edward J. Smith, a very experienced and respected sailor. This was going to be his final voyage before a well-earned retirement . . .

MAIDEN VOYAGE

At noon on Wednesday, 10 April 1912, the *Titanic* had set off from Southampton harbour to cross the Atlantic. A band played, and the quayside was lined with cheering crowds waving off the greatest ship ever built. The passengers, including some of the world's richest people, were looking forward to the voyage. The ship was fitted out in the grandest style, with a theatre, tennis courts, a swimming pool, gardens, a billiard hall, a ballroom and even a Turkish bath – everything they could possibly wish for.

Iceberg ahead!

For four days, the voyage went peacefully. On the morning of Sunday, 14 April, as the ship steamed across the North Atlantic, passengers strolling on deck noticed large lumps of ice floating in the sea. Several other ships in the area sent radio warnings of icebergs drifting further south than was usual for the time of year. By nightfall, it was very cold. But Captain Smith ignored the warnings and gave orders for the ship to speed up.

The gymnasium on board the *Titanic* (above)
The luxury liner's grand staircase (left)

THE GREATEST SHIP

The Titanic *was the largest passenger liner of its day. It weighed 46,329 tonnes and was 260 metres long. Its nine decks were as high as a ten-storey building, and each of its four huge funnels was big enough to drive a train through. The engines were driven by twenty-nine huge boilers and 159 furnaces. There were 915 crew. The cost of a one-way ticket for a first-class suite of rooms – the height of luxury – was an astonishing 4,350 dollars.*

At about 10 pm, another warning came in, but the radio operator was busy sending messages for the passengers, and he may not have passed this vital information to the captain. At 11.40 pm, a look-out noticed something large looming ahead – a gigantic iceberg. Minutes later, the ship was swung hard to one side, the engines were put into reverse, and the ship swung back again. But it was much too late – the iceberg had ripped a gaping hole in the *Titanic*'s side.

A tragedy at sea

The shock of the collision was so small that it hardly disturbed anyone on board. Passengers on the upper decks did not even wake up. The captain stopped the ship and sent sailors to look for damage, but nothing could be done – water was already pouring into the lower decks. An SOS signal was sent from the radio room. Then Captain Smith ordered the crew to uncover the lifeboats so that the women and children could get into them. The passengers watched in disbelief. Many were still in evening dress. How could the invincible *Titanic* be sinking?

When it was the men's turn to leave the ship, there were not enough lifeboats to go round. As the band carried on playing, the *Titanic* sank. At 2.20 am, the great ship's lights went out forever. The *Titanic* turned on one end and plunged deep beneath the waves. Many of the people who were still on board jumped into the water or desperately tried to cling to the wreckage. Those who fell into the freezing ocean did not last long. Altogether, 1,490 people died that night, including the captain, who went down with his ship. Just 711 survivors were picked up from the lifeboats a few hours later. It was the worst shipwreck there had ever been during peacetime. Since then, nobody has ever claimed that a ship is unsinkable.

At about 2.20 am on Monday, 15 April, RMS *Titanic* turned on its end and sank.

FINDING THE TITANIC

For more than seventy years, the wreckage of the *Titanic* lay 3,965 metres down on the sea bed in the North Atlantic Ocean. In 1985, the American oceanographer Dr Robert Ballard and a team of scientists from the Woods Hole Oceanographic Institute in the USA, together with a French salvage company, began to search for it.

In August 1985, the team were on board their research ship, *Knorr,* in the middle of the north-west Atlantic. They were running out of time, and the weather was becoming worse. Their remote-controlled underwater camera boat, called *Argo,* was exploring the sea floor and sending pictures back to the ship. But so far it had found no sign of the wreck. With only five days to go, things were looking bleak. Then, just after midnight on 1 September, one of the *Titanic*'s massive boilers appeared on the on-board video monitor. *Argo* had found the *Titanic*! The wreck lay in two pieces on the sea bed. Had it broken in two as it sank?

Bollards used for mooring ropes, now turned to rust

Exploring the wreck

A year later, in July 1986, Ballard returned to the wreck site on board a new research ship, *Atlantis II*. This time he was going to dive down to the wreck himself, inside *Alvin*, a submersible (a type of mini-submarine), and would try to land on the ship's deck. On *Alvin* there was another remote-controlled robot camera, *Jason Junior*, which would be used to explore inside the wreck. It took nearly two and a half hours for *Alvin* to drop through almost 4 kilometres of water. As they descended, the water became colder and blacker. It was getting cold inside the submersible, too. But more problems were to come. *Alvin*'s sonar had stopped working, and without it they could not see or navigate. What was more, water was leaking into the battery banks that powered the submersible. Ballard could risk staying only a very short time on the sea bed. He strained his eyes to see through the porthole, and there it was. *Alvin*'s lights showed the massive steel hull of the *Titanic* rising up in front of them! It was just a brief glimpse, and then *Alvin* had to go back to the surface.

On board the submersible *Alvin* was a remote-controlled robot camera, *Jason Junior*, which was used to explore the inside of the *Titanic*.

A dream come true

Once *Alvin* had been repaired, Ballard made a second dive. This time, he and his team could clearly see the rust-covered bow, with the huge anchors still in place and unbroken glass in the portholes. The wooden decks had rotted away. The next day, Ballard landed by the edge of the *Titanic*'s grand staircase, a sad reminder of the ship's fabulous luxury. More surprises were in store. Using *Jason Junior*, the team were able to see a huge chandelier, almost perfectly preserved, and to peer inside several of the first-class cabins. It was like exploring a ghost town. Before he left the wreck for the last time, Ballard placed a plaque on the tangled wreckage of the *Titanic*'s stern, in memory of all the people who died on that terrible night in April 1912.

Resting in peace

Many people believe that the wreck of the *Titanic* should lie undisturbed, as the grave of the people who died. Not everyone agrees. One of the strangest twists in the *Titanic* story took place in August 1996, when an American salvage company spent over three million pounds trying to raise part of the wreck from the sea bed. The company brought along 1,700 tourists, including three survivors of the tragedy. Before their eyes, the cables snapped, and a 15-tonne section of the ship plunged back into the sea, where many people feel it should be left in peace.

TITANIC TREASURES

There have been rumours that the Titanic *was carrying five million dollars' worth of diamonds, as well as many other precious items, including a rare, leather-bound book, the* Rubaiyat of Omar Khayyam, *studded with over a thousand precious stones. Many of the passengers were very rich, so they must have had jewellery and other valuable possessions with them. These treasures have never been found. They were locked inside the ship's safes when it sank. Although Ballard found one of these safes (shown below) and turned its handle with* Alvin's *mechanical arm, its door would not budge – it had rusted shut.*

39

Unsolved Mysteries

Only a selection of shipwrecks and sunken cities are described in this book. There are many more lurking beneath the waves – some bursting with treasure, and all full of information about the past. Some are lost forever, and their secrets are safe from prying eyes. But divers and fishermen keep on making wonderful finds, by accident or as the result of careful research. Some of these discoveries raise more questions than they answer . . .

According to legend, a volcanic eruption or earthquake caused terrible floods which drowned the city of Atlantis. But no ruins have ever been found.

The Lost Land of Atlantis

In about 380 BC, the Greek writer and philosopher Plato wrote about a great island in the Atlantic Ocean which, in the space of a day and a night, sank without trace beneath the sea. The island was called Atlantis, and it is the most famous lost land of all. Today, we are no nearer finding out what happened to this legendary island than Plato was more than 2,000 years ago.

According to Plato, Atlantis lay to the west of the Pillars of Hercules (the Straits of Gibraltar) in the Atlantic Ocean and was 'larger than Libya and Asia put together'. It was a powerful kingdom, whose army conquered large parts of Europe and Africa, until eventually it was defeated by the Greeks. The people of Atlantis were wise, noble and virtuous. Plato also described the main city, which was circular and built around a large hill. Here stood the king's magnificent palace, together with a fabulous temple dedicated to Poseidon, god of the sea, which was covered in silver, gold and other precious metals.

Atlantis – fact or fiction?

The story goes that, one day, violent earthquakes and floods struck the city, and it sank without trace. Plato believed that the people had become greedy and dishonest, and that this was the gods' way of punishing them. But what really happened? Did Atlantis even exist? If it did, where do its ruins lie?

Ever since Plato's time, people have been fascinated by Atlantis, and have written hundreds of books about it. In the nineteenth century, an American, Ignatius Donnelly, wrote an amazing book, *Atlantis, the Antediluvian World*. Donnelly did not just believe that Atlantis existed; his idea was that it was the very first civilization, the home of the first human beings. He agreed with Plato that a natural disaster had destroyed the city, but he had no evidence to back up his story.

The throne room in the palace of Knossos, on the Greek island of Crete. Could this have been the site of Atlantis?

Where was Atlantis?

Since then, there have been many theories about Atlantis, some sensible and some very strange. People have suggested that it was in all sorts of places, from the Azores and the Bahamas to Greenland and the Sahara Desert. In the 1960s, a Greek archaeologist said that the gigantic volcanic explosion which blew apart the island of Thera (Santorini) and Crete in 1500 BC may also have destroyed Atlantis. Excavations on these islands have revealed the remains of large houses, decorated with beautiful wall-paintings, like the ones Plato described. Some of these wall-paintings show the sport of bull-leaping, which the King of Atlantis was said to enjoy. Could one of these islands be Atlantis? We shall never know. In 1975, experts met up at the University of Indiana, in the USA, to discuss whether Atlantis was fact or fiction. They decided that it was fiction. But even experts can make mistakes!

LYONESSE – THE LOST KINGDOM

In the sea about 10 kilometres west of Land's End, the southernmost tip of England, lie the Seven Sisters rocks. Legends say that they mark the site of Lyonesse, a great kingdom which once linked Cornwall to France. According to these stories, in the fifth century AD a huge wave swept over Lyonesse, and it vanished beneath the sea. There was only one survivor, a man called Trevellyan, who rode his horse to safety on high ground. In the centuries since then, fishermen have often hauled up pieces of doors and windows in their nets, and these are said to come from Lyonesse. But no trace of the kingdom itself has been found so far. Did Lyonesse ever exist? Do its ruins lie on the sea floor? No one knows for sure.

Rocks off Land's End, Cornwall

THE RIDDLE OF THE LUSITANIA

It was 1 May 1915, and Britain and Germany had been at war for nine months. That morning, an advert appeared in the New York papers. It warned travellers intending to travel across the Atlantic to Britain that the ocean was a war zone, and that ships flying the British flag were in danger of being destroyed by German submarines. It was signed by the Imperial German Embassy.

On the same day, the RMS *Lusitania,* a British ship, set sail from New York for Liverpool. Most of the passengers had read the advert, and they knew about the dangers. But none of them dreamed that Germany would actually carry out its threat and attack an unarmed passenger steamer. The *Lusitania* was one of the biggest, fastest and safest liners there were. It had been built in 1907, and was the pride of the Cunard line. Its owners described it as a 'floating palace'. As it steamed out of port, with its passengers crowding the decks, it looked indestructible. A week later, it lay at the bottom of the Atlantic Ocean.

The *Lusitania* was sunk off the south coast of Ireland. It now lies, hundreds of metres down, on the bed of the sea.

Submarine strike

The Germans suspected that the *Lusitania* was carrying an illegal cargo of weapons and ammunition across the Atlantic, which made it a fair target. In fact, this was true, but the passengers knew nothing about it. To reduce the risk, the ship's captain, William Turner, had strict orders to cross the Atlantic as quickly as possible, changing direction frequently so that the ship would not be an easy target. Turner ignored these commands. The *Lusitania* sailed at well under its top speed, and steered a straight course. Off the south coast of Ireland, Turner slowed the ship down even more. At 1.40 pm on 7 May, a German U-20 submarine, captained by Lieutenant Karl Schweiger, fired a torpedo which struck the *Lusitania* on its side. It took only eighteen minutes for the 30,000-tonne ship to go down, taking 1,198 of its 1,959 passengers and crew with it.

RMS *Lusitania*, the pride of the Cunard line

What really happened?

For many years, people believed this story. But several mysteries were never solved. How could just one torpedo sink such a massive ship? Why did it go down so quickly? Did the ammunition on board explode when the torpedo struck? Divers who explored the wreck said that a huge hole had been blasted in the ship's side.

In 1993, the American oceanographer Robert Ballard led an expedition to the wreck site, in the hope of finding some answers. He sent down his remote-controlled underwater robot, *Jason,* fitted with cameras and lights, to photograph the damage.

But, to his surprise, when *Jason*'s cameras filmed the ship's hull, there was no sign of a large hole! So what was it that sent the *Lusitania* to its watery grave? Did the ship's gigantic boilers burst when the torpedo struck? Or was the blast caused by an explosion of coal dust as the torpedo hit the coal bunkers? (Coal was used to power the ship.) We shall probably never know. The truth about the *Lusitania* remains as dark and murky as the water where the wreck now lies.

Early divers exploring and photographing the wreck of the *Lusitania*

SUNK WITHOUT TRACE

In the last thirty years, at least 100 ships and planes have disappeared, in calm weather and for no obvious reason, in a stretch of the Atlantic Ocean known as the Bermuda Triangle. They simply vanish, without warning, and without even having time to radio for help. No bodies or wreckage have ever been found. So what makes them disappear? People have suggested various explanations: attacks by modern-day pirates, magnetic force fields, or whirlpools sucking ships down. There is even a theory that the ships are hijacked by underwater UFOs! The mystery continues . . .

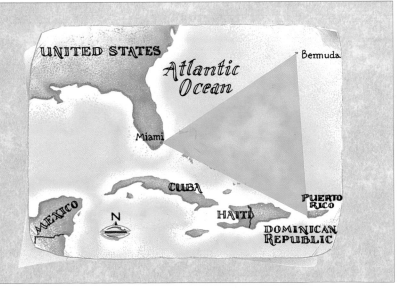

43

GLOSSARY

Archaeology The study of human history by examining remains and ruins such as shipwrecks, burial sites and ancient cities

Artefact An ancient object

Astronomer A scientist who studies the stars, planets and other heavenly bodies in space

Breakwater A huge stone wall built out from the land into the sea to break the force of the waves hitting the coast

Broadside When all the guns down one side of a ship are fired at once

Crannogs Ancient houses built on artificial islands in the middle of lakes, marshes and bays

Dredger Equipment used for lifting objects from the mud and silt of the sea bed

Echo sounders Instruments used to explore the sea bed. They give out bleeping sounds, which hit objects on the sea bed and send back echoes. The shape of the objects can then be identified from these echoes

Estuary The mouth of a large river where it flows into the sea

Galleon A large Spanish warship or treasure ship

Hercules A hero of Ancient Greece. He was enormously brave and strong, and wore a cape made out of the skin of a magical lion for protection.

Hull The main body of a ship

Marine To do with the sea

Pewter A grey metal made from a mixture of tin and lead or other metals

Porcelain A type of very fine pottery

Salvage To save a ship or the cargo it carries after the ship sinks or runs aground

INDEX

THE TITANIC

THE NUESTRA SENORA
DE ATOCHA

PORT ROYAL

CHICHEN ITZA